Doulce memoire

Publications of the Early Music Institute

Thomas Binkley, general editor

Doulce memoire

A STUDY IN PERFORMANCE PRACTICES

George Houle

WITH TWENTY-FOUR VERSIONS
OF THE CHANSON

INDIANA UNIVERSITY PRESS
Bloomington and Indianapolis

Manufactured in the United States of America

Library of Congress Cataloging-in-Publication Data

Doulce mémoire.

  (Publications of the Early Music Institute)
  Bibliography: p.
  1. Music--16th century. 2. Chansons, Polyphonic.
3. Sandrin, fl. 1538-1561. Doulce mémoire. 4. Perfor-
mance practice--16th century. I. Houle, George.
II. Sandrin, fl 1538-1561. Doulce mémoire. 1990.
III. Series.
MT6.5.D68 1990   89-753543
ISBN 0-253-38846-5 (pbk.)

  1 2 3 4 5 94 93 92 91 90

To Glenna

Contents

Performers' Parts
(parts needed simultaneously are printed on separate pages)

Contents

Doulce memoire

Introduction

The chanson *Doulce memoire*, by Pierre Regnault, "dit Sandrin" (ca.1490-1561), is justly famous. Its beautiful and simple melodic line is elegantly wedded to poetry that evokes nostalgia for something that almost everyone has experienced--a consuming, passionate love that no longer exists except in bittersweet memory. The chanson begins plainly and eloquently, mounts to an emotional climax, and then concludes in calm resignation.

The poetic text was published among the works of Clément Marot, but in the sixteenth century the poem was sometimes attributed to François I, King of France, who was imprisoned in Italy after the battle of Pavia in 1525,[1] and *Doulce memoire* would have been understood as his lament for his distant kingdom.

Sandrin's four-voice setting of this text was so pleasing and well received that it was frequently reprinted and became the subject of many arrangements, intabulations, parody masses, and contrafacta over a span of ninety years. These versions make *Doulce memoire* available to a variety of performers and ensembles. The music is presented with its original note values and barlines, but written in score or transcribed from tablature. This preserves many aspects of the original notation and makes it accessible to modern performers. Singers and instrumentalists will find versions of two, three, five, and six parts, lutenists may choose from seven intabulations that vary in difficulty, and gambists have available idiomatic literature for their instrument that ranges from Diego Ortiz's intriguing and well-constructed versions through some dazzling and virtuosic viola bastarda ornamentations. There are keyboard arrangements from the simplest intabulation by Ammerbach to an elaborate fantasy by Hernando de Cabezón. The present collection of versions of *Doulce memoire* is intended to make one of the most popular chansons of the sixteenth century readily available to musicians.

The arrangements for lute preserve the chanson with particularly valuable performance indications since chromatic inflections of pitch, *musica ficta*, are precisely indicated in lute tablature, which indicates where to place the fingers on the instrument rather than what notes to play. *Musica ficta* was supplied by performers reading staff notation through training and experience rather than through notation symbols. Tablatures and arrangements for instruments also introduced ornamental variations into the music, thus recording an individual performer's personal interpretation of the chanson.

This study is based on the thirty-six versions of *Doulce memoire* listed in the Bibliography. These offer the opportunity to investigate many facets of performance practice in the sixteenth century. Musical theorists and performance manuals of the period give us much valuable information, but there is more to know that can be learned only from the music itself. With the help of these versions of *Doulce memoire*, it will be possible to augment what the theorists offer--for instance, to resolve contradictions between various possible chromatic inflections and to know more precisely where and when to introduce ornamentation.

This study profits from the work of various music historians and performers. Howard Mayer Brown's study of the theatrical chanson in France shows that *Doulce memoire* was widely quoted in plays, and his bibliography lists over fifty publications of this chanson.[2] Brown has summarized instructions on

1. Frank Dobbins, "*Doulce memoire* A Study of the Parody Chanson," *Proceedings of the Royal Musical Association* 96 (1969): 85-99.

2. Howard Mayer Brown, *Music in the French Secular Theater, 1400-1550* (Cambridge: Harvard University Press, 1963), pp. 207-208.

ornamentation from the performance manuals of the sixteenth century[3] and shown how a study of lute intabulations can cast light on editing and performing the music of Josquin des Prez.[4] Frank Dobbins's "*Doulce memoire*, A Study of the Parody Chanson" discusses the history of the text as well as different musical settings of Sandrin's melody. His study lists several versions of the melody to which different texts have been set. Veronica Gutmann has considered three ornamented settings of the chanson as typical examples of Renaissance ornamentation practice.[5]

Solmization

In the sixteenth century, musicians were taught how to distinguish pitch and recognize intervals through solmization, a system that linked syllables and pitch relationships, that is the equivalent of modern *solfeggio*. In his English translation of Ornithoparcus's *Micrologus*, John Dowland identifies solmization as a method of learning music:

> Every Song may be sung three manner of wayes: that is, by solfaing, which is best for Nouices, that learne to sing: By sounding the sounds only, which belongs to Instrumentists, that they may affect the mindes of them that heare or conceiue them with care or solace: Thirdly, by applying, which is the worke of the Cantor, thatso he may expresse Gods praise.[6]

Dowland's "nouices, that learne to sing" may mean beginners or possibly singers learning a new piece. In either case the pitches of any composition would be explicitly or implicitly understood in terms of solmization, rather than the octave-based note letters *a, b, c,* etc., in modern use.

Solmization cannot be regarded as an unknown or even esoteric discipline today, and the article in *The New Grove Dictionary of Music* by Andrew Hughes gives a good account of the theory and general practice of solmization in the Renaissance. However, the actual use of the hexachord *ut, re, mi, fa, sol, la* may not be familiar to performers, even those interested in sixteenth-century music. Learning the practice of solmization is valuable in that it enables one better to understand the music in its original terms.

Three hexachords were the basis of the system: the <u>natural</u>, from c (*ut*) to a (*la*); the <u>hard</u>, from g (*ut*) to e (*la*); and the <u>soft</u>, from f (*ut*) to d (*la*). The hard hexachord contains a "hard" b (*mi*), b-natural, which is indicated by the familiar square-shaped natural sign. The soft hexachord uses a "soft" b (*fa*), b-flat, indicated by a flat sign. Many melodies move beyond the range of one hexachord, necessitating mutation to the syllables of an adjacent hexachord. One must know how to choose between the soft and hard hexachords when mutating, and for this the signature of the part is the best guide. The soft hexachord is chosen whenever there is a b-flat in the key signature and the hard when there is none.

3. Howard Mayer Brown, *Embellishing 16th-Century Music*, Early Music Series 1 (Oxford and London: Oxford University Press), 1976.

4. Howard Mayer Brown, "Accidentals and Ornamentation in Sixteenth-Century Intabulations of Josquin's Motets," in *Josquin des Prez: Proceedings of the International Josquin Festival-Conference held at the Juilliard School at Lincoln Center in New York City, 21-25 June 1971*, edited by Edward E. Lowinsky in collaboration with Bonnie J. Blackburn (London: Oxford University Press), 1976, pp. 475-522.

5. Veronika Gutmann, "Improvisation und instrumentale Komposition: zu drei Bearbeitungen der Chanson 'Doulce memoire,'" in *Alte Musik Praxis und Reflexion. Sonderband der Reihe Basler Jahrbuch für Historische Musikpraxis* (Zurich: Amadeus Verlag, 1983), pp. 177-86.

6. John Dowland, *Andreas Ornithoparcus his Micrologus, or Introduction: Containing the Art of Singing* (London: Thomas Adams, 1609; modern edition, New York: Dover, 1973) Liber I, Chap. 5, p. 14.

Each hexachord repeats the same relationship of intervals: *ut-re*, tone; *re-mi*, tone; *mi-fa*, semitone; *fa-sol*, tone; and *sol-la*, tone. The pattern is symmetrical, a semitone in the middle with whole steps on either side. *Mi-fa* always indicates a semitone.

Since the hexachords overlap by two or three notes, there are various points at which a mutation may be made. One can find Renaissance documentation to support different systems, but as all of them work we will use the one advocated by John Dowland and Ornithoparcus in learning *Doulce memoire*. The following table of mutations gives this system:

In ascending the gamut, mutations are made to *re* of the higher hexachord. From the natural to the hard hexachords (a fifth apart), the singer moves from *sol* to *re* (replacing *la*), and from the hard to the natural hexachords (a fourth apart), *fa* to *re* (replacing *sol*). In descending, mutations are made to *la* of the lower hexachord. Therefore, from the hard to the natural hexachord the singer descends from *mi* to *la* (replacing *re*), and from the natural to the hard, *fa* to *la* (replacing *mi*). This places one in the lower part of the new hexachord in rising (without using *ut*, which is not euphonious to sing) and in the upper part of the new hexachord in moving down the scale. The mutations between natural and soft hexachords are similar, with the difference being that the soft hexachord is a fourth higher than the natural, and the natural a fifth higher than the soft.

An example of a mutation occurs in the superius of *Doulce memoire* after letter G. The e will be sung *mi* in the natural hexachord, and then the line rises past *la* of that hexachord. In accordance with Dowland's chart, the a will change to *re* in the hard hexachord and continue to *sol* on the high d. During the octave leap down to d, there will be a mutation back to the natural hexachord with *re*.

mi fa sol re mi fa   sol   fa   sol   re   mi   fa sol sol   fa mi la   sol   la

Between letters I and J, the superius requires three hexachords, beginning on *fa* (= c in the hard), mutating to *la* (= a in the natural), again mutating to *la* (= e in the hard) and continuing to *re* before leaping up to *sol-fa-sol* at J, and ending in the hard hexachord.

Some practice quickly acquaints the beginner with stepwise melodies, and rarely does the range of any voice in a sixteenth-century composition require more than the compass of two hexachords. By locating the mutations between two, or at most three hexachords, one will be prepared to perform a part. Singing intervals, especially leaps of a fourth or a fifth, requires more practice since a number of these leaps will occur between hexachords. Singing octaves by using adjacent hexachords requires that the singer change syllables. For instance, the octave C to c must be sung *ut/fa*, rather than *fa/fa* or *ut/ut*, both of which imply the omission of an entire hexachord. The hexachord system therefore teaches a singer to recognize repetitions of pitches at the intervals of the fourth and fifth as well as at the octave.

Modes

A singer can recognize the modes through solmization, as the syllables identify modally significant intervals, that is, the particular fifths and fourths into which modal octaves are divided. There are four different species of fifths. The Dorian fifth, d to a, is solmized *re-la* in any hexachord; and the order of the scale steps within the Dorian fifth is implied by the syllables *re (mi-fa-sol)* to *la*. Similarly, the scale steps within the Phrygian fifth, *mi-mi*, the Lydian, *fa-fa*, and the Mixolydian, *ut-sol*, are distinctive. The four modes added to the traditional eight by Glareanus use fifths already identified with other modes; both the Æolian and Dorian fifths are *re-la*, and the Ionian fifth is *ut-sol*, the same as the Mixolydian.

There are only three species of fourths, which when added to the fifths, either above or below, complete the modal octaves. In authentic modes the fifths are under the fourths, and in plagal modes the fifths are above. The lowest note of the fifth is always the *finalis* of the mode. The Dorian fourth is solmized *re-sol*, the Phrygian fourth *mi-la*, and the Lydian *ut-fa*. The Mixolydian mode must reuse the Dorian fourth, *re-sol* to complete its octave, and because of this, Gaffurius does not recognize a plagal Mixolydian, although most other theorists do.

The first step in learning a part in a composition is to locate the pitch of the first note in a hexachord. Some theorists, such as Sebald Heyden, give elaborate directions for assigning a syllable to the first note.[7] The purpose of such directions is to assure the placement of the initial syllable in the hexachord that will best accommodate the the tones to come. For example, in solmizing the tenor part at the beginning of *Doulce memoire*, if a begins on *la* of the natural hexachord the melodic descent to *re* is easily accommmodated. This phrase outlines the Dorian fifth, which is expanded to the full Dorian octave when the tenor leaps to d (*sol*) and descends through the Dorian fourth from *sol* to a (*re*).

The tenor is the organizing, or mode-bearing, voice of the composition and was recognized as such by most theorists of the Renaissance. It is the tenor that shows the clearest outline of modal intervals, and therefore the mode of the composition.

---

7. Sebald Heyden, *De arte canendi* (Nürnberg, 1540), translated by Clement Miller, pp. 37-40.

Musica Ficta

Accidental inflections of notated pitches were added to music in customary ways. It is somewhat as if notation employed abbreviations that must be spelled out in performance. Inflections can be categorized as those required (1) by signatures, (2) by canon and imitation, (3) to avoid *mi contra fa* in melodic perfect consonances, (4) to avoid *mi contra fa* in intervallic perfect consonances, and (5) by cadential inflections.[8] We shall mainly be concerned with the last three of these categories as we examine *Doulce memoire*.

Tritones and diminished fifths are discordant intervals that are identical in sound but distinct in their notation. In general they were prohibited during the fourteenth through sixteenth centuries, although they were tolerated in special circumstances. They were identified through their solmization, and the rules by which they were corrected are given in terms of solmization syllables.

The solmization syllables *mi* and *fa* lie in the middle of every hexachord, and when the *mi* of the hard hexachord (b-natural) is followed by the *fa* of the natural hexachord (f), or vice versa, the resulting interval is the tritone, or diminished fifth, which is jarring, awkward, and hard to sing. *Fa* of the soft hexachord followed by *mi* of the natural produces the same interval.

The unpleasantness of this interval is corrected by lowering the *mi* a semitone. By placing a flat symbol in front of it, this note becomes solmized as *fa* rather than *mi*. Thus the "hard" hexachord is turned into the "soft." While it seems that Renaissance musicians might as well have corrected this interval by raising *fa* by a semitone into a *mi*, this was not mentioned as an alternative.[9]

Another melodic situation that usually identified a clash of *mi contra fa* and required an alteration of pitch occurred when the melody line went only one note above *la*, the highest note in a hexachord. The extra note was sung *fa*, a semitone above *la*, regardless of the pitch indicated, according to the following rule:

> Toutesfois & quantes que par dessus ces six voix s'en trouuera vne seule n'excedante
> que d'une seconde, elle s'appellera fa, sans faire muance, laquelle faudra profferer molle-
> ment mesmement sans aucun signe de b mol, pourueu que celuy de # dur n'y soit mis.[10]

> Whenever a note exceeds the six degree-syllables by a second, this seventh note must
> be called fa without making mutation into the next hexachord. This note must be sung flat
> (mollement) even in the absence of any flat sign before or above it, unless the natural #
> sign were to affect it.

Thus the hexachord was extended upward by one note without a mutation by placing b-flat instead of b-natural above the natural hexachord, and e-flat above the soft. Since the hard hexachord already had *fa* (f) one note above *la* (e), no chromatic change occurred in that position. Karol Berger shows that this "rule" is really a consequence of the *mi contra fa* prohibition and was understood as such by capable musicians.[11] Nevertheless, the rule came to have something of an independent existence apart from the avoidance of the *mi contra fa* problem that it was intended to correct.

There are two places in the tenor part of *Doulce memoire* where a hexachord is exceeded by one note. The first is between letters B and C. If the a following the rest is sung *la*, the quarter-note b will become *fa*, b-flat.

---

8. The most authoritative discussion of this is in Karol Berger's *Musica ficta: Theories of Accidental Inflections in Vocal Polyphony from Marchetto da Padova to Gioseffo Zarlino* (Cambridge: Cambridge University Press, 1987). The following discussion is indebted to this book and the insights of its author.

9. Berger, pp. 80-84.

10. Maximilian Guilliaud, *Rudiments de Musique Pratique* (Paris, 1554), quoted in Gaston Allaire, *The theory of hexachords, solmization and the modal system* (Rome: American Institute of Musicology, 1972) p. 45.

11. Berger, p. 78.

re   la   la   la   fa la sol fa sol   fa   sol

The second is after letter D. At the beginning of the new phrase, the a can be sung *la*, and the two b's between the a's would then become *fas*.

mi   re   la   fa   fa   la   fa   sol la   re   re   mi

These two examples are ambiguous in their solmization since the initial a of each phrase has been sung immediately before as *re* in the hard hexachord. In each phrase a mutation must be made sooner or later from the hard to the natural hexachord. No theorist has indicated precisely where the change should be made. If a mutation to *la* were made at the beginning of the phrase, the b would become *una nota supra la*. If the mutation were made when the line descends to *ut/sol* (g) in the middle of the phrase before letter C, the b would remain *mi*.

We must turn to the lute intabulations for more precise information. Of twelve intabulations,[12] eight use b-flat after letter B. From this we can surmise that a mutation to the natural hexachord was made at the beginning of the phrase. This suggests that mutations might best take place at the beginning of a phrase even though the mutation is required only at some later point. Four of the twelve intabulations use b-natural at this place.

After letter D, five intabulations use b-flat and seven use b-natural. It might seem that the use of b-flat in the cadence at letter E would be a consequence of using b-flat in the tenor immediately after letter D, but nine of the twelve intabulations use b-flat in the cadence at letter E, and only three keep the b-natural. No conclusion can be drawn from this contradictory evidence.

The altus invites an appliction the rule of one note above *la* between letters I and J, where there is only a passing-tone *mi contra fa* conflict with the tenor. If one blindly followed the rule of using *fa* whenever a hexachord is exceeded by one note, b-flat would be used, even though there is no serious conflict of *mi contra fa*. In the same twelve sources, two omit the altus part at that point, and only four use b-flat. Six indicate a b-natural and therefore support the conjecture that the *una nota supra la* rule is intended to identify a possible conflict of *mi contra fa*, and need not be followed if there is no problem.

Another category of *musica ficta* is employed in order to avoid vertical conflicts of *mi contra fa* in perfect consonances. These difficulties are mainly tritones and diminished fifths, but also include imperfect octaves and unisons. An example can be found in the superius part before letter F on the word "seul," where there is a b one note above *la* of the natural hexachord.

– voir   Rom —   —   pant le   but de ma seul' es– pe — ran –ce

12. Lute tablatures by Phalese (1549), Teghi (1547), Heckel (1552), Drusina (1556), de Rippe (1562), Phalese (1568), and Waissel (1573); a cittern tablature by Vreedman (1570); keyboard tablatures by Ammerbach (1583), Cabezón (1578), and Jan z Lublina (1548); and Ortiz's ornamentation (1553).

In Ortiz's *Trattado de glosas* this b is notated # to warn that it should not be altered. *Fa* cannot be introduced here because it would sound against a *mi* in the tenor and make a diminished octave. This is easily determined by someone reading from score, but the part-reading performer is aided by the sign.

Two untexted manuscript copies of Sandrin's *Doulce memoire* contain some but not all of these *musica ficta* alterations which were introduced in order to avoid the conflict of *mi contra fa*. Basel Ms. FX 17-20 includes the b-flats in the tenor after letters B and D, and the altus b-flat in the codetta. The b-flat after D suggests that both altus and bassus would continue to use b-flat to the end of the phrase, which would bring about a Phrygian cadence at letter E. Regensburg Ms. 940/41 includes a b-flat in the bassus immediately before letter E, and a b-flat in the altus in the codetta. The only *musica ficta* concern of the copyists of these manuscripts appears to have been the avoidance of *mi contra fa*.

Alterations are used to insure diatonic smoothness and to identify the modes clearly, rather than to introduce chromaticism. By listening carefully we may be able to hear whether these altered notes clarify the meaning of the words and project the emotional qualities of the mode.

The Text

The poetic structure, the intended message, and the meaning of the words are of fundamental importance to both singers and instrumentalists. What inflections to introduce and how to make proper cadences and cadential ornaments are determined by careful consideration of the text.

The poem is identified by Dobbins as "a decasyllabic *huitain* with the three-rhyme scheme of abab bcbc (with alternating feminine and masculine endings) common to many of the eight-line epigrams of the time."[13] This results in an alternation of ten and eleven syllables per line. Sandrin's setting of the first line separates *memoire* from *en plaisir*, thus requiring twelve syllables to be enunciated instead of eleven. If the text were only spoken, the mute *e* at the end of *memoire*, would be elided.

> *Doulce memoire en plaisir consomée*
> *O siecle heureux qui cause tel scavoir.*
> *La fermeté de nous deux tant aymée*
> *Qui à nos maux a su si bien pourvoir.*
> *Or maintenant a perdu son pouvoir*
> *Rompant le but de ma seul esperance,*
> *Servant d'exemple à tous piteux à voir.*
> *Fini le bien, le mal soudain commence.*

> Sweet remembrance of consumate pleasure,
> O happy time that has left such memory;
> The strength of our great love,
> Which provided so well against our troubles,
> Now has lost all of its power;
> The destruction of my only hope,
> Serves as example to all, piteous to see.
> Good ends and suddenly evil begins.

Only the last seven syllables of lines 1 and 3 and the last line of the poem are repeated. With these exceptions, each line is set with a single musical phrase that culminates in a cadence. Lines 3 and 4 repeat the musical setting of lines 1 and 2. The musical form may be diagrammed as A B A B C D E F F (codetta). The setting is primarily syllabic; however, in line 8 a melisma underlines the pathos of the con-

---

13. Dobbins, p. 87.

clusion of the poem. The musical rhythm and the poetic rhythm of the phrases are closely and harmoniously integrated.

The Choice of Mode

Sandrin's faithful treatment of the structure of the poem is well matched by his choice of the Dorian mode. Many theorists describe its rich affective associations. According to Gioseffo Zarlino:

> Il primo modo ha un certo mezano effetto tra il mesto, & lo allegro per cagione del Semitono, che si ode nel concento sopra le chorde estreme della Diapente, & della Diatessaron; non havendo altramente il Ditono dalla parte graue; per sua natura e alquanto mesto. Pero potremo ad esso accommodare ottimamente quelle parole, le quale saranno piene di grauita, & che trattaranno di cose alte, & sententiose; accioche l'harmonia si conuenghi con la materia, che in esse si contiene.[14]

> The first mode has a certain medium effect between sad and cheerful because of the minor third in the concentus on the two extreme notes of the fifth and the fourth [i.e., a and d], and, as it doesn't have a major third in the low register it is by nature somewhat sad. However by use of accidentals it can accommodate words that are full of gravity and deal with lofty sentiments, and the harmony can adjust to the meaning of the words.

A composer's choice of mode establishes the emotional framework for a composition by drawing on associations common to musicians and their audience. Sandrin matches this poem contemplating the loss of love with a mode that is "by nature somewhat sad." Since performers today cannot rely on having an audience that is familiar with modal associations, it is doubly important that the spirit and nuance of the chanson convey the appropriate affect.

Cadences

In order for the poetic line to be sung forth clearly it must be appropriately punctuated. A cadence is the musical equivalent of grammatical punctuation in most musical styles, including those of the sixteenth century, but musicians understood the cadence differently then. According to theorists of the time, cadences were considered a contrapuntal movement from imperfect to perfect consonances. From the time of Marchetto da Padova (fl. 1305-26) to that of Gioseffo Zarlino (1517-90), theorists advised that imperfect consonances must lie as close as possible to the perfect consonances that they approach. Cadences are produced by two voices and accompanied or augmented by the progression of the other parts. Minor thirds between cadential voices are closest to the unison, one voice moves by a semitone the other by a tone. Similarly, major thirds between cadential voices move to the fifth, and major sixths to the octave. A minor sixth must be altered to major if it is to resolve properly to the octave, and a major third must be altered to minor in order to resolve to a unison. It was necessary for a performer to recognize where an alteration was required to make a cadence, and also to know when a cadential progression should not be made. According to Zarlino:

> A cadence is a certain simultaneous progression of all the voices in a composition which accompanies a repose in the harmony or the completion of a segment of the text upon which the composition is based. Or we might say that it is a termination of a part of

---

14. Gioseffo Zarlino, *Le Istitutioni harmoniche* (1558), Part IV, chap. 18, p. 320.

the concentus--at a midpoint or at the end--to divide the portions of the text. And since the cadence is very necessary in harmonies, its lack deprives the work of an essential ornamentation needed for definition of the parts, as well as of the text. It should not be used unless the end of a clause or period of the prose or verse has been reached; that is, only at the end of a section or part of a section. The cadence has a value in music equivalent to the period in speech, and could well be called the period of the composition. It is found also at resting points in the harmony, i.e., where a section of the harmony terminates, in the same way that it marks the pauses in the text, intermediate and final. Nor is its location [pitch] always the same; but in the interest of grateful pleasing harmony, its location is changed and varied. The text conclusion should coincide with the cadence, and not on an arbitrary tone, but on the proper and regular tones of the mode used.[15]

Zarlino has this to say about the progression from the major sixth to the octave:

> Nature, which has jurisdiction over everything, has so designed that not only those with musical training but the unschooled and even farmers--who sing after their own fashion, without reasoning about it--are accustomed to progress from major sixth to octave, as if nature had taught them. . . . To make the rule easy to follow, every progression from imperfect to perfect consonance should include in at least one part the step of a large semitone, expressed or implied. To this purpose the chromatic and enharmonic steps will be found very useful. . . . [16]

Cadences may take place on any degree of the scale, regardless of whether the unaltered tones of the scale produce the necessary major sixth to octave, or minor third to unison. The location of the cadence, the pitch, and its relation to the mode are all factors that reflect intermediate and final divisions in the text as reflected in the music.

Cadences to intervals other than the unison and octave are possible but regarded as imperfect:

> To make intermediate divisions in the harmony and text, when the words have not yet reached a final conclusion of their thought, we may write those cadences which terminate on the third, fifth, sixth or other similar consonance. Such an ending does not result in a perfect cadence, rather the cadence is said to be evaded. It is fortunate that we have such evaded cadences, for they are useful when a composer writing a beautiful passage feels the need for a cadence, but cannot write a cadence because the period of the words does not coincide."[17]

It is clear that the performer has a choice as to whether to perfect imperfect cadences, he may supply an accidental inflection that makes a semitone out of a tone, or make no change at all.

The next consideration is how intervals of a cadential progression are altered when they are not in close proximity to the tones to which they resolve. Cadential accidentals are usually sharps, whereas *mi contra fa* is almost exclusively corrected by flats. The most frequent cadences are those on the final degrees of the four modes; therefore a c-sharp is required for the Dorian mode, an f-sharp for the Mixolydian mode, and no alteration for the Phrygian and Lydian modes. The Lydian cadence ascends a semitone from e to f, *mi* to *fa*, diatonically. The Phrygian cadence is exceptional because the semitone progression is in the descending voice, from *fa* to *mi*.

---

15. Gioseffo Zarlino, *The Art of Counterpoint*, Part III of *Le Istitutioni harmoniche* (1558), translated by Guy A. Marco and Claude V. Palisca (New York: Norton, 1976), chap. 53, pp. 141-42. See also Berger, pp. 129-30.

16. Zarlino, *The Art of Counterpoint*, chap. 38, p. 83.

17. *Ibid.*, chap. 53, p. 151.

Cadences to other pitches are less frequent but occur through modal transposition or as cadences to scale degrees of a mode other than the *finalis*. Cadences to c, as the *finalis* of the transposed Lydian mode, require no alteration. A cadence to a might be to the *finalis* of the transposed Phrygian mode, or to the *confinalis* of the untransposed Dorian mode. A Phrygian cadence to a requires a descending semitone from b-flat to a, *fa* to *mi*, but the cadence on the Dorian *confinalis* a will require g-sharp ascending to a, *mi* to *fa*. The most frequently used cadential sharps are f, c, and g, and the most frequently required flats, for correcting *mi contra fa*, are b, e, and a. Only the potential conflict of a need for a-flat and g-sharp requires a decision about tuning.[18]

Zarlino tells us that the perfect cadence will end on a major triad, which represents harmonic proportionality. The minor triad, which is the result of arithmetic proportionality, is considered less perfect.

> Diligent examination of the consonances arranged according to the one and the other methods will reveal that the arithmetical order--that resembling the arithmetical proportion--is somewhat removed from the perfection of harmony, because its elements are not arranged in their natural locations. On the other hand a harmony resulting from harmonic division or resembling it is perfectly consonant because the parts of this division are collocated and ordered according to the natural sequence of the sonorous numbers.[19]

This requirement of ending on a major harmony was first discussed about 1520 by Pietro Aaron, in *Toscanello in musica*, and subsequently confirmed in the writings of Lanfranco, Vanneo, and Vicentino.[20]

Zarlino states that the regular cadential tones in the Dorian mode are d, f, a', d'.[21] The lowest pitched d is the *finalis* of the mode, the lowest note of the modal fifth, and thus the predominant tone in the mode. The upper note of the fifth, a, is next in importance, and is known as the *confinalis* or reciting tone. F, the mediant tone, contributes the minor third that gives the Dorian so much of its characteristic sober nature; and d is the octave of the *finalis*, and of relative unimportance. The order in which Zarlino mentions the regular cadence tones seems to be a reflection of their importance in the modal hierarchy. Other tones are irregular, therefore of even lesser consequence. We shall see that the cadences on c in *Doulce memoire* rank low. They occur on an irregular tone and are introduced by movement of the subsidiary contratenor and bassus voices instead of by the structurally important soprano and tenor voices.

Musical Structure

As we examine Sandrin's setting in the light of these considerations, both modal and cadential, we see that the 8 lines are paired, weak-strong, with line eight given special emphasis by the use of cadences and repetition. The division between the two halves of the poem is evident because of the musical repetition of the first quatrain.

The relative modal importance of the tones on which cadences occur helps to establish the structure of the chanson. At letter A there is an avoided cadence on d, the caesura that results emphasizes the first two words and sets them apart from the rest of the line. The cadence at the end of the first line (letter B) is on a, the dominant of the mode, but an appended repetition of the words *en plaisir consomée* cadences weakly on c (letter C) in the bassus and contratenor voices. The cadence at the end of the second line of the poem is strong, between tenor and superius, and arrives on a, the dominant of the mode (letter D). Since the third and fourth lines are repeated to the same music, each pair of lines in the first quatrain has equal weight.

18. See Berger, pp. 139-54.

19. Zarlino, *The Art of Counterpoint*, chap. 31, p. 71.

20. Berger, pp. 138-39.

21. Zarlino, *The Art of Counterpoint*, chap. 31, p. 71.

In the second quatrain, the cadence of line 5 (letter E) takes place between bassus and contratenor, by resolving to a. The cadence of line 6 (letter F) takes place between tenor and superius by resolving to a. The cadence to line 7 (letter G) between bassus and contratenor resolves to c. Line 8 has three cadences: the first (letter H) to d', the octave of the *finalis*; the second (letter I) to a; and the third (letter J) to d, bringing us to the modal *finalis*. These last three cadences are all between the tenor and the superius. The repetition of the line and the musical setting is exact (with cadences at letters K, L, and M). The pedal note and final phrase, which repeat the words *le mal soudain commence* after letter M, leads to a weighty and somber conclusion on the *finalis*.

None of the published part-book settings of Sandrin's composition include chromatic alterations by sign. The cadences indicated by the notation, except for the weak and irregular cadences to c, are represented by minor sixths that expand to octaves on a (letters B, D, E, F, I, and L) or on d (letters H, J, K, and M). It is up to the performer to carry out Zarlino's instructions that proper cadences should replace these minor sixths if the meaning of the words requires such punctuation.

A Comparison of the Sources with the Rules

But what did they do? Does this information give us enough insight to understand what was done by sixteenth-century musicians? The performance choices of a number of musicians are preserved in tablatures for lute, cittern, and keyboard that specify precise pitches and add ornamentation, much of which is cadential decoration. It is conceivable that a performer might not always follow the tablature, but the notation does give a version of the composition thought by the intabulator to be definitive. Let us investigate the changes that occurred to the uninflected vocal lines of *Doulce memoire* when arranged in tablatures.

Lute Tablatures

Lute tablatures give insights to performance practice that are quite different from those arising from the notation of vocal part-books. Tablatures present the full score to the eye and include accidental inflections and ornamentations. Ornamentation was often improvised by singers and instrumentalists in the sixteenth century, and styles of ornamentation were idiomatic, within a generally accepted tradition, to instruments as well as to individual performers. Not all the ornaments of lute tablatures are applicable in singing or to other instruments. The first two measures of lute versions of *Doulce memoire* have ornamentation that gives the effect of a crescendo, but singers ornament these measures best by augmenting their sound.

Two categories of ornamentation can be distinguished in tablatures: the embellishment of beginnings and middles of phrases, and cadential ornaments. Although the use of formulas can be found in phrase ornamentation, in general quick-moving conjunct *passaggi* or diminutions that are freely melismatic are employed. Dissonances usually occur on passing tones and auxiliary notes, and only rarely are there appoggiaturas or accented dissonances of any kind.

Cadential ornamentation, by contrast, is primarily formulaic and decorates the suspension dissonance and its resolution. The usual formula, called *groppo* in Italian treatises, repeats the suspension and its resolution several times, then moves to the note of resolution with a turn: 8 7, 8 7, 8 7 6 7, 8. Variations on this formula abound in the tablatures, but the basic melodic progression is clearly derived from the *groppo*. The cadential ornament may be more or less elaborate and use longer or shorter note values, or the *groppo* may merge imperceptibly with phrase ornamentation approaching the cadence.

Phrase ornamentation in lute tablatures does not always follow a single melodic part. Often the *passaggi* will seem to decorate several lines and move from one to another in quick running notes. Sometimes the entire range of the chanson, from bass to treble, will be filled with these running divisions. This all-encompassing ornamentation is common to the lute and to keyboard instruments. It is less frequently done on the viola da gamba or by a singer, and then it is given the name *alla bastarda*. We shall consider the viola bastarda and its style as seen in several versions of *Doulce memoire* later on. Ornamentation in lute tablatures can be illuminating to performers other than lutenists because there are many more complete and fully realized ornamented versions of sixteenth-century compositions in intabulations than there are in vocal or instrumental instruction books.

Carminum quae chely 1549)

Lute intabulations in the early sixteenth century did not attempt to include all the voice parts of the original composition, as later intabulations did. The lute tablature of *Doulce memoire* in Phalese's *Carminum quae chely vel testudine canuntur* of 1549 is not the earliest published lute version, but it is perhaps the most old-fashioned because it omits the contratenor part entirely. It is of particular interest to us because it illustrates how Zarlino's theoretical principles may be put into practice. The tablature organizes the chanson clearly and chooses to make chromatic alterations and to introduce ornaments in only a few of the possible locations. The cadences to c, already of lesser importance, are diminished further by the omission of the contratenor, one of the cadential voices. The cadences to a are subtly varied; those at letters B, L, and I remain minor sixths progressing to octaves; they are not proper cadences at all, and have no ornamentation. Cadences at letters F and D remain minor sixths, both have cadential *groppi*, but the one at letter D is the more elaborate.

The progression at letter E is made into a Phrygian cadence, and the concentus to which the sixth resolves is altered to A major, a dramatic effect. This evokes the emotional associations of the Phrygian mode for the words *Or maintenant a perdu son pouvoir*:

> che habbia natura di commovere al pianto; la onde gli accommodarano volontieri quelle parole,che sono lagrimeuoli, & pieni di lamenti.[22]

> [The Phrygian] has the nature of moving to tears; it goes well with words that cause weeping, such as laments.

The principal cadences to the *finalis* at letters J and M are marked by both major sixths and ornaments.

22. Zarlino, *Le Istitutioni harmoniche*, Part IV, chap. 20, p. 324.

The lesser cadences to d at H and K resolve intervals of major sixths but have no ornaments.

There are two additional chromatic alterations because of cadences. The c-sharp in tactus 3 seems to be preparing a cadence to d at letter A, but a rest in the superius makes this an evaded cadence. Because of this interrupted cadential formula, the words *doulce memoire* are separated from the poetic continuation of the line, and the evaded cadence provides a musical caesura. The second chromatic inflection is an f-sharp in the last concentus of the chanson, which provides a satisfying musical finality.

There is, however, one alteration that doesn't clarify the verse-oriented structure. This is found at tactus 23, where a cadence has been made in the middle of the poetic line by introducing a c-sharp and a *groppo* in the tenor. Otherwise, the verse structure of the poem has been carefully followed in this tablature.

Other tablatures make other cadential choices but still interpret the structure of the poem through musical punctuation. Many sources supply *musica ficta* for all potential cadences. Ten of twelve versions introduce the requisite g-sharps or c-sharps on every occasion for cadences from the beginning through letter H.

For cadences at letters H and J, on the first time through line 8 of the poem, most introduce *musica ficta*, but at letters K and M all sources are unanimous in making all cadential inflections. Accidentals are not found at letters I and L in all the sources. It seems that performers from mid-century on have taken to heart Ornithoparcus-Dowland's advice:

> Euery Song is so much the sweeter, by how much the fuller it is of formall closes. For so much force there is in Closes, that it maketh Discords become Concords for perfection sake. Therefore let Students labour to fill their Songs with formall Closes.[23]

A cadence (or formall Close) may be enhanced in two other ways: by introducing an ornament, or by resolving the cadence to a concentus with a major third. Cadential ornaments are found more frequently at the ends of lines 2, 4, 6, and 8 of the poem, and more frequently on a repeat than on the first time through.

A cadential resolution to a chord altered to have a major third is employed more selectively than is the introduction of a cadential ornament. The cadence marking the end of the fifth line of the poem at letter D is made major in nine out of twelve sources, making this cadence the most important one in the first half; only four sources give a major resolution to the chord at letter B. At Letter E eleven sources indicate a cadence with a descending semitone in the bass. This resolves to a major third in ten sources and to a plain octave in one. The resolution to a major third marks it as a strong cadence, one that attracts our attention, even though the cadential voices are subsidiary parts, the contratenor and bassus. The cadence of the sixth line, paired with the fifth, is also given strength through a resolution to a major chord in ten sources and with ornaments in eleven. The cadence at letter G, which resolves to c, is ornamented in eight sources. The last line of the poem has many cadence points in order to mark its importance, and although there are many cadences and almost as many ornaments at letters H, I, J, K, and L, the finality of letter M and the even greater finality of the codetta are ensured by the prior resolutions being to minor thirds or plain octaves. The codetta ends on a major chord in nine sources, on an octave in one, and on a minor chord in two.

Both of the tablatures in which the codetta ends on minor chords deserve attention because they seem to contradict Zarlino's association of major with greater perfection and finality. In Drusina's tablature, on the last line of the chanson, the performer is directed by a sign at letter K to return to letter H and then to end at letter J. There is no codetta and no sign to change the minor third at J. Perhaps performers would initiate the change to major on their own in order to create a more definitive conclusion.

Pierre de Teghi, *Des chansons et Motetz* (1548)

In the tablature of Pierre de Teghi, the final cadence at letter J is to the interval of an octave and a fifth. This sound has adequate theoretical perfection to terminate a composition but sounds rather empty in the harmonic context of *Doulce memoire*. Hearing the empty octave and fifth, the listener is left in suspense about whether the more final ending to come will have a major or a minor chord. In the codetta the tablature alternates g minor with d major chords, only to slip into d minor on the last chord. This is quite unexpected and seems inexplicable until we investigate the next chanson in the tablature, Pierre Certon's *Fini le bien*, a companion piece or *réponse* to *Doulce memoire*. The minor, incomplete sound at the end of Teghi's *Doulce memoire* seems intended to link the two chansons. It is possible that if a composition ends on a minor triad, a sixteenth-century audience would expect a continuation.

In five tablatures the codetta has f-sharps in the tenor and b-flats in the altus, with the result that there are parallel minor thirds between the voices. Zarlino objects:

---

23. Dowland, Liber IV, chap. 5, p. 85.

> It is forbidden to place two perfect consonances of the same species consecutively, it is
> the more forbidden to write two imperfect ones of the same proportion, because these are
> not so consonant as the perfect.[24]

In four tablatures there are f-sharps in the tenor, and the b is unchanged in the altus; thereby the logic of Zarlino's rule is obeyed.

Pierre de Teghi's tablature includes one feature not found in any other lute version of *Doulce memoire*. An instruction at the beginning of the tablature tells the player to tune the lowest course of the lute one tone lower, that is, to F instead of G, in order for this note to be sounded when approaching the cadence at letter J.

Wolff Heckel, *Discant Lauttenbuch* (1552)

Wolff Heckel's German tablature introduces no chromatic inflections until D, at which point there is also an elaborate ornament that emphasizes the importance of this cadence. Approaching letter E, the voice leadings are altered, almost garbled, in order to cadence with the bass descending by leap from e to A. The d in the superius against the e in the bass is a strong and accented dissonance not quite rationalized by its resolution to c-sharp and b. Apparently Heckel wished to avoid the Phrygian cadence, but he was unable properly to alter the voices to make any other kind. A cadence with an ornament and a major-triad resolution occurs at letter F, and the one at letter G has an ornament, but the remaining cadences are weak, so that only the codetta conveys finality. There, d minor gives way to major by a chromatic half-step in the tenor, and parallel minor thirds occur between tenor and altus until the final d-major chord. Heckel's tablature seems weak in its musical craftsmanship as well as in its violation of Zarlino's more subtle rules.

Benedict de Drusina, *Tabulatura* (1556)

Another German tablature, by Benedict de Drusina, is also less skillful than the those of Italian players. Voice leadings are sometimes quite incomplete, and occasionally a part is left out when it is inconvenient for the lutenist. Drusina has included more non-cadential ornamentation, usually steadily moving, mainly stepwise eighth notes. At the cadence at letter D, a *groppo* in eighths leads to a long string of eighth-note diminutions that extend to letter E. The cadence at D is the strongest before the final cadences at letters J and M. These have been altered to contain major sixths progressing to octaves and have more elaborate *groppi* than at D.

Albert de Rippe, *Tiers livre de tablature* (1562)

Albert de Rippe's tablature is quite elegant and presents Sandrin's setting idiomatically arranged for the lute. Many chords are arpeggiated in a somewhat syncopated style, showing the performer precisely what to do with sustained harmonies. De Rippe's style is very close to the *style brisé* of seventeenth-century French lutenists. The subsidiary parts are often omitted when an elaborate ornament is to be played, so that the player can concentrate on the quick notes. All cadences to a and d are anticipated by ascending g-sharps or c-sharps, except at letter E, where there is a Phrygian cadence that resolves to a major chord. The important cadences at the end of lines 4 and 8 are given simpler and slower-moving ornaments than those at subsidiary cadences. This reversal of the usual procedure is quite effective in conveying the shape and affect of the chanson.

---

24. Zarlino, *The Art of Counterpoint*, chap. 29, pp. 62-63.

Phalese, *Luculentum Theatrum* (1568)

This setting contains some of the written-out lute arpeggiation of de Rippe's tablature. Whenever possible, cadences are approached by major sixths, and distinctions between them are made by resolutions to major chords and more elaborate ornaments at important cadences. The ornamentation of this tablature includes much more passage work than it does cadential ornamentation. The sheer amount of ornamentation has increased with each of the tablatures we have considered, from Heckel, Drusina, de Rippe, to the *Luculentum Theatrum*.

Matthaeus Waisselius, *Tabulatura* (1573)

The most elaborately ornamented lute tablature is that of Matthaeus Waisselius, his version is overlaid with an almost continuously running stream of eighth notes. The cadences are sometimes distinguished from the eighth-note diminutions by their moving in sixteenth notes. The structure of the chanson seems more obscured than clarified by this virtuosic display of ornamentation.

Cittern Tablatures

A tablature for the cittern by Sebastian Vreedman is of interest because of the way the chanson is adapted to the narrow range of this instrument, both plebian and popular in the sixteenth century. Even though it is transposed up a fourth and deprived of all notes below tenor g, the outline of *Doulce memoire* is clear and the cadences emphasize the poetic structure of the chanson as effectively as the lute tablatures. Since the lower strings on large citterns were doubled at the octave, the bass would have an increased resonance not represented by the transcription. The harmonies are closely confined within a narrow compass, and there are odd voice leadings and chord positions that stem from the limitations of the instrument.

Keyboard Tablatures

Ammerbach, *Tabulaturbuch* (1583)

Ammerbach's transcription is quite simple. It reproduces Sandrin's four-voiced setting with little change except for adding cadential chromaticism. All cadences have major sixths that resolve to octaves, including the unpoetic cadence at tactus 23. A hierarchy of important points is maintained by resolutions to major triads at letters D, F (a questionable choice on textual grounds), and J and at the end of the codetta. The repeat of the last section is indicated by a sign instead of being written out. In the codetta, Ammerbach provides both f-sharps for the d chords and b-flats for the g chords.

Hernando de Cabezón

Hernando de Cabezón's keyboard intabulation of *Dulce memoriae* is a virtuoso ornamentation for keyboard comparable to Waissel's lute tablature. The *passaggi* maintain a continuous eighth-note rhythm, with occasional sixteenth-note *groppi* and flourishes, through the written-out repeat of the first half of the chanson. In the second half, ornamentation in quarter notes, triplet quarters, and eighth notes accelerates to a climax of sixteenth notes between letters H and I, followed by an intricately syncopated triplet eighth-note passage between K and L. The codetta is omitted. Structural ranking of cadences marking the ends of lines of the text is maintained by the use of a major triad at letter B (first time) but a minor one at letter D (first time), minor at B (second time), and major at letter D (second time). At letter E there is a Phrygian cadence to a major chord, and the cadence at letter F resolves to a minor chord. There is a cadence at tactus 23 (without textual justification), and the cadences at letters H and I resolve to minor chords. At letter J the cadence resolves to an octave d, but passage work supplies an f-sharp later in the measure. Letter K has a minor chord, L has a major chord, and the final cadence resolves to a major triad after a suitably elaborate ornament. Cabezón's version can be admired for its intricacy and brilliance of figuration and for preserving the structure of *Doulce memoire* with care and sensitivity.

Jan z Lublina (1537-48)

Jan of Lublin's *Doulce memoire* organ tablature comes from the opposite corner of Europe. In this manuscript, cadences do not mark the structure of the chanson as clearly as in other versions, and often the ornamentation seems to obscure structural points. Letter A does not have an avoided cadence, letter E has no cadence, and all repetitions and the codetta are suppressed. The cadences to c at letter C and G are minimally marked; all others have cadential groppi and raised leading tones, with resolutions to minor triads on a and d. Perhaps Jan worked without the text when making the intabulation, but in any case this intabulation is one of the least satisfying versions of the chanson.

Diminutions

Six versions of *Doulce memoire* are found in three different ornamentation manuals. One of the best-known sixteenth-century manuals is Diego Ortiz's *Trattado de glosas*,[25] which contains four *recercadas* on *Doulce memoire* for the viola da gamba. Writing about these and other ornamentations, Veronika Gutmann[26] distinguishes four kinds of diminutions. Her first category is the diminution of an individual part, usually the superius or the bassus, or the successive diminution of different individual parts. This category is illustrated by Ortiz's first, second, and third *recercadas* on *Doulce memoire*, of which the first and third ornament the lowest voice, with occasional upward leaps to sound a phrase from one of the middle parts or even the superius. The second *recercada* is a melodic ornamentation of the superius. Gutmann's second category of diminution is one that adds an additional part to the composition. This is illustrated by Ortiz's fourth *recercada*, which adds a fifth voice that duplicates the harmonies but not the counterpoints of the chanson. The third category is a diminution that follows several voices of the composition simultaneously, and no ornamentation of *Doulce memoire* exists to illustrate this practice. The fourth category is ornamentation *alla bastarda*. We will be examining several examples of this style later.

Ortiz's barlines are preserved in this edition, and they are interestingly irregular. Where little or no ornamentation is added, there are fewer barlines and the performer can read the music much as it is in vocal part books. When the ornamentation is elaborate, more barlines are introduced to guide the performer's eye through the quick notes. The result of this notation for us is that the ornamented sections seem vigorously and irregularly organized, and we must remember that sixteenth-century performers did not equate barlines with accentuation.

Musica ficta remains the same in all four of Ortiz's *recercadas*. All cadences to a and d are supplied with leading tones, and a cadential hierarchy is established by resolutions to major thirds in only two places: at letter E, after a Phrygian cadence; and in the codetta, after an initial resolution to the minor chord at letter M. All flats suggested by solmization rules are indicated by sign except for the altus's b-flat in the codetta. A c-sharp introduced one breve before letter K, in anticipation of the cadence, creates an augmented fifth with the bass, a forbidden interval and an unexpected sound in this style. In other places, linear direction in the ornamentation brings about some unusual clashes between contrapuntal lines, for example, one breve after letter H and one breve before letter M.

---

25. A modern edition of Ortiz's *Trattado* was issued by Bärenreiter in 1936, edited by Max Schneider.
26. Gutmann, p. 177.

Girolamo Dalla Casa's *Il vero modo di diminuir* (1584) contains the first ornamentation *alla bastarda* for the viola da gamba. This style presents a technical challenge to the player who must encompass all vocal ranges of sixteenth-century music, from bass to treble, on the bass viola da gamba. It is a virtuosic art to ornament *alla bastarda*, and the viola da gamba enjoyed such a considerable repertoire in this style that it was known as a *viola bastarda* when playing such ornamentation.[27] Dalla Casa's *bastarda* ornamentation is a school-book exercise in sixteenth-note triplets, called "treplicate," which displays little of the musical fantasy and technical brilliance that characterizes most viola bastarda music. This arrangement jumps from one voice to another and adds relatively slow-moving ornamentation, except for the occasions when the ear is treated to a burst of quick "treplicate," the longest group of which fills the time of seven quarter notes. This diminution does nothing to clarify the structure of the chanson.

An ornamentation by Vicenzo Bonizzi is among the most brilliant examples of viola bastarda music and perhaps the most dazzling display piece based on *Doulce memoire*. Bonizzi states in his preface that he accompanied the virtuoso gambist Oratio Bassani at the keybord, and his ornamentations were inspired by these performances. The diminution leaps from part to part transforming everything it touches. Between letters C and D, and even more elaborately on the written-out repeat of the same passage, the harmonic framework is decorated by patterned arpeggios. There are brilliant passages of thirty-second notes between letters G and H and in the final flourish. Bonizzi evolves rhythmic patterns in some sections which recur later, thus giving a hint of structural coherence in the diminution--for example, syncopated sixteenth notes after Cc, which return after letter G. However the coherence of the ornamentation is not based on the structure of the chanson, and indeed, it is not carried out with sufficient consistency to establish more than tantalizing reminiscences of the melodic line in the mind of the listener.

Arrangements

Several arrangements of the four-part chanson for two, three, and six voices from collections devoted to transcriptions of well-known melodies illustrate the use made in the sixteenth century of *Doulce memoire* as a popular tune. The arrangements all use the poetic text and the melody of the superius from Sandrin's setting, but only Jacques Buus's six-part arrangement uses the other contrapuntal lines of Sandrin's chanson as well. The chanson melody quoted in these arrangements does not include any of the chromatic alterations encountered in the tablatures.

Two-Part Arrangements

These easy and pleasant duets for singers or instrumentalists are quite simple and may have been conceived as counterpoint exercises. They can be studied as samples of improvisation that show how to add another voice to a well-known melody. The codetta was omitted from the two-part versions, and some phrases of the superius were altered or omitted. The earliest, simplest, and best of the two-part settings is by François de Layolle, who invented a new counterpoint above the melody. Layolle's skill is evident in the clever cadences and rhythmic liveliness of the counterpoint, which moves quite freely and alludes to the melody through short motives. Not all of the original cadences are retained; some are evaded or rhythmically overridden contrapuntally. The cadences that are retained provide a coherent structure; cadences at D and its repeat, and those at letters G, H, I, J, L, and M are all strong.

Pierre de Manchicourt introduced some alterations of the melody, which is in the upper voice transposed up a fourth, although frequent imitation between the parts places phrases of the melody in the lower voice. There is a modest ornamentation of the melody on the repeat of the first half.

---

27. See Jason Paras, *The Music for Viola Bastarda*, edited by George Houle and Glenna Houle (Bloomington: Indiana University Press, 1986).

More imitation between the voices is found in Gardane's setting, which keeps Sandrin's phrases as the basis for new counterpoints. There is little rhythmic contrast between the voices, and subordinate and major cadences are treated alike.

A Three-Part Arrangement

The three-part setting by Josquin Baston is a small masterpiece. The voices have an intricate contrapuntal relationship, and there is a special harmonic color that arises from the many Phrygian cadences. Several of these cadential progressions are caused by approaching e, the penultimate note of the descending cadential voice, by leap from b-flat, *fa* to *mi*. To avoid this tritone the e must be changed to e-flat (*fa*); then the cadence descends by semitone from e-flat to d. In other places Baston has indicated the Phrygian cadence directly by accidentals. This setting apparently retains the Dorian mode, transposed to g, but borrowings from the Phrygian are so strong as to give the chanson the mournful quality of that mode more than the sober quality of the Dorian.

A Six-Part Arrangement

The arrangement by Jacques Buus, by contrast, is grandiose. Buus was organist at San Marco in Venice, which may help to explain his love of color and sonority. A canon based on the tenor part of the chanson, and moves in slower note values than the other parts, is traded between the cantus and tenor parts. Melodic motives from the chanson are used as the subjects of Buus's counterpoints. The conclusiveness of any of the cadences is diminished by their many repetitions, the density of the writing, and the sonority of the six parts. Each of the voices except bassus I has an opportunity to introduce the upward-moving semitone in a cadential formula. Some poor counterpoint, with scarcely concealed parallel octaves, can be found in the inner voices between tactus 11 and 12, but the rich sonority minimizes this technical deficiency. The fullness of the sound is most noticeable in the codetta phrase, with the d major ending sounding bright and strong.

Contrafactum: Another Formal Structure

Thus far we have examined arrangements in which the musical structure reflects the poetic form of Marot's text. A contrafactum of *Doulce memoire*, the last section of the *Magnificat primi toni* by Clemens non papa, uses Sandrin's music with a different text. The cadential structure, as Zarlino prescribes, is therefore completely different. Clemens uses the superius melody and other vocal parts of the chanson as the basis of the composition and invents a fifth voice, somewhat like the ornamented part in Ortiz's fourth *recercada*. Like many "extra" voices, such as contratenor parts in fifteenth-century chansons, the fifth voice has an erratic melodic outline instead of the smooth, mostly stepwise motion characteristic of Sandrin's counterpoints. One of the functions of the fifth part in Clemen's *Magnificat* seems to be to prevent chromatic alterations at points where cadences occurred in the chanson. At the cadence preceding letter B the added voice doubles the g in the superius at the octave, preventing a cadential g-sharp. A cadence at letter D is similarly prevented, so that the first strong cadence is delayed until the equivalent of tactus 25 of the chanson, where formerly there was no cadence. In Clemens's *Magnificat* these twenty-five tactus set the words *sicut erat in principio et nunc et semper*, and the remainder of the melody sets *et in saecula saeculorum, amen,* which is repeated many times. Cadences are prevented at the equivalents of letters H, I, K, and L in order to emphasize the cadences at letters J and M. Clemens's cadences appropriately reflect the new words in the structure of the piece.

Parody Masses

Two masses that use *Doulce memoire* as the basis of their melodic material also associate the familiar phrases with different words. The *Missa ad imitationem moduli Doulce memoire* by Orlando di Lasso quotes the full contrapuntal texture of many phrases but never uses the complete melody of the chanson. Cipriano de Rore's *Missa super dulcis memoria* employs the melody and counterpoints of the chanson and uses associations between chanson text and mass text in almost every phrase that is meant to color our understanding. For example, the *Christe* begins with the music of *en plaisir consommée*, and the next occurrence of *Christe* uses the melody of the chanson superius from letters B to C, now altered with an f-sharp. The warmth of the d-major triad, which unexpectedly changes the quotation, is most striking. Zarlino's characterization of imperfect consonances assures us that sixteenth-century musicians heard the change from minor to major with some of the same emotional connotations we have today:

> The property or the nature of the imperfect consonances is such that some of them are lively and cheerful, accompanied with great sonority; and others, although sweet and smooth, tend to be sad and languid. The former are the major third and sixth, with their compounds; the latter are the minor forms. All these have the capacity to alter every composition and to make it sad or cheerful, according to their respective natures."[28]

Other associations of chanson phrases with words of the mass are also appropriate, such as setting *Jesu Christe* to *ma seul esperance* and *Domine Deus, Agnus dei* to *servant d'exemple a tous piteux a voir*. However, sometimes the unspoken words of the chanson contradict those that are sung, as in the unsettling pairing of *Pater omnipotens* with the music of *a perdu son pouvoir*.

In de Rore's mass, Sandrin's rather sober melody is infused with both warmth and grandeur to give us one of the most richly rewarding artistic transformations of this chanson.

Conclusions

The versions of *Doulce memoire* that we have examined allow us to suggest some answers to questions that arise among performers as well as among historians:

(1) To what extent do rules from learned theorists describe the performance of practical musicians?

(2) Does ornamentation contribute to the musical logic of a composition, or is it rather an irrational decoration that arises from pure fantasy and abundant technique?

(3) Do solmization rules and formulas have an independent authority for performers, or do they merely implement more fundamental rules?

We can begin to answer the first question by considering the particular rules of structure and performance that have been illustrated by these versions of *Doulce memoire*. Zarlino, the learned theorist, strongly links musical form and text: cadences are considered to be musical punctuation modelled on the lines, phrases, and sentences of poetry. In the old-fashioned tablature of *Carminum quae chely vel testudine canuntur*, some potential cadences are overlooked in favor of others, a practice close to what Zarlino describes as desirable. The other tablatures make almost every potential cadence into a major sixth expanding to an octave. This is equivalent to punctuating every clause, phrase, and sentence of a text alike. His idea that cadences should lend subtle shape to the form seems to be largely disregarded.

Not all cadences are identical in their voice leading, although the sixth is usually made major by raising the ascending voice so that it moves by a semitone. A choice can be made between this and lowering the

---

28. Zarlino, *The Art of Counterpoint*, chap. 10, p. 21.

descending voice a semitone when the cadence resolves to a. Theory states that this is the case, and the performance sources of *Doulce memoire* confirm it.

Although cadential progressions are consistently made into major sixths that resolve to octaves, they are varied in finality by whether they resolve to a plain octave or fifth, or to a minor or a major chord. The performer's choice of interval or chordal third in the resolution becomes important in outlining the musical form.

Cadential ornamentation, the *groppo* and its variants, emphasize the formal design of the music. The performer has a number of options to consider: whether to ornament, to ornament simply or elaborately, or to merge the cadential ornament with a preceding phrase ornamentation. The performer's fantasy must be engaged, and his or her performance technique must easily surmount the demands encountered, but clear logic is the guide.

Consequently, while the means that are used to delineate musical structure are not those specified by Zarlino, his advice that cadences must reflect the form of the text is followed in most of the versions of *Doulce memoire* we have investigated.

Zarlino's prohibition of parallel similar thirds, an extension of the prohibition of parallel fifths and octaves, is ignored by many performers. Some versions take care to alternate major and minor thirds, but many tablatures revel in successions of minor thirds, for instance, in the codetta. They produce a harmonic intensity that seems to please many of the lutenists.

The second question, whether ornamentation contributes to the musical logic of a composition, has been partially answered in regard to cadential ornamentation. Not all ornamentation is cadential, and therefore we must consider what conclusions are to be drawn from non-cadential ornamentation included in the tablatures.

Phrase ornamentation may heighten the expressiveness of certain phrases or figures. Singers can make a crescendo on the first notes of *Doulce memoire* that cannot be done on the lute, but the addition of a few ornamental notes in the bass part in the first measures of the chanson gives an equivalent rise in intensity. However, ornamentation of the entire phrase is an opportunity to display virtuosity of technique and imagination more than cool logic. In the most exuberant ornamentations there is a point, which is difficult to determine precisely, when virtuosity and brilliance obscure the structure of the chanson. Ornamentation then becomes freely decorative, depending on pure fantasy and abundant technique, and delighting in a dazzling display.

This results in a changed esthetic sensibility. As balance, unity, and proportion underly the Renaissance artistic canon, disturbed balance, approximation, and confused formal outline define a mannerist esthetic. Several versions of *Doulce memoire* are truly manneristic, such as those of Matthaeus Waissel, Hernando de Cabezón, and Vicenzo Bonizzi. In these, "proportion breaks down and experiment takes the form of morbid ingenuity or scalding wit; art and thought curve away unpredictably on private tangents. . . ."[29]

Another aspect of mannerist sensibility might be found in the pairing of *Doulce memoire* melodies and counterpoints with new words. These new words are necessarily shadowed by the more familiar ones lodged in memory. Substance and shadow may be in agreement, but in the parody masses there are uneasy moments when the two are in conflict. The possibility of intentionally ironic, mocking, or irreligious contradictions is quite conceivable. This must have been a delight to the mannerist!

The third question is whether solmization rules and formulas have an independent authority for performers, or do they merely implement more fundamental rules designed to avoid tritones and other discordant intervals and to produce proper cadences? An important and consistent inflection in these sources is the addition of a flat in order to avoid *mi contra fa*. This validates the doggerel Latin solmization rule that *mi contra fa est diabolus in musica*.

Another rule, to sing *fa* when there is only one note above *la* in a hexachord, sometimes causes a "correction" to be made when there is no *mi contra fa* to correct. Only about half of the places where this sol-

---

29. Wylie Sypher, *Four Stages of Renaissance Style* (New York: Doubleday, 1955), p. 102.

mization is encountered, without there being a conflict of *mi contra fa*, are altered. Therefore it would seem that many, but not all, performers introduced *musica ficta* according to fundamental concepts rather than solmization rules-of-thumb.

Karol Berger has concluded that "most accidental inflections in music of our period, whether notated or implied, do belong unambiguously to the domain of invariable musical text, but some clearly do not and are a matter of variable performance."[30] Most accidentals are so firmly fixed by intention and tradition that they are part of the fundamental idea of the work; therefore, as with abbreviations in a written text, a performer realized the part from recognizable indications, not out of his or her fancy at the moment of performance. Thus we should expect to find most performance versions, such as lute tablatures, in agreement on accidental inflections, and this is generally the case.

Berger identifies only two kinds of inflections that cannot be implied: signature accidentals; and "authorial" accidentals, which are totally unorthodox and must be specified by the composer or an editor. In Sandrin's chanson, there are no authorial accidentals; and signature accidentals (of one flat) are found in only two arrangements, the two-part *bicinia* by Pierre de Manchicourt and the three-part version by Josquin Baston. In both of these the reason for the signature is that the melody is transposed a fourth higher. Josquin Baston's lovely arrangement goes beyond a signature accidental and includes some authorial accidentals, specifically the e-flats in the tenor (the lowest sounding voice) in measures 11, 23, 47, 57, and 62 and in their repeats. The other e-flats in the tenor part are required by the convention of avoiding *mi contra fa*, and notating them is only cautionary. The category of authorial inflections is well illustrated by this example, as the mode and consequently the affect of *Doulce memoire* are altered. Baston's arrangement stands apart from the other versions of *Doulce memoire* as a significantly different composition.

Another authorial inflection is the quite unexpected major triad introduced by Cipriano de Rore in the *Christe* of his *Missa super dulcis memoria*, which alters the phrase between letters B and C of the chanson. The transformation of the dour and sober Dorian mode by this warm major chord dramatizes the emotional spirit that infuses this section of the mass. The chanson does not raise any expectation of this harmony, only an unconventional inflection may accomplish it, and from this we experience the power of chromaticism that goes beyond the more conventional uses of *musica ficta*.

Doulce memoire is a musical creation of great charm and haunting beauty. The fascination it had for sixteenth-century musicians is evident from its many arrangements, its several printings, and the long span of its popularity. The versions of *Doulce memoire* on the following pages are compositions that confidently await their re-creation in a new age. A performance that embodies sixteenth-century perceptions of order and technique will have nuances and meanings subtly different from one that is based on today's concept of form and performance techniques. The variety of interpretations of this chanson that we have seen may inspire us to greater extravagance as well as to greater simplicity within a range of possibilities that we are only beginning to understand.

30. Berger, p. 168.

Doulce memoire

TWENTY-FOUR VERSIONS
OF THE CHANSON

Le Parangon des Chansons 1538

Doulce Memoire

Pierre Regnault dit Sandrin

Carminum quae chely vel canuntur 1549

Des chansons et motetz   Teghi   1547

Lute

Discant Lauttenbuch   Wolff Heckel 1552

Lute

Tabulatura   Drusina 1556

Tiers Livre de Tablature de Luth   Albert de Rippe 1562

Luculentum Theatrum Musicum   Phalese 1568

Tabulatura   Waisselius   1573

Nova longeque elegantissima cithara   Vreedman   1568

44

Tabulaturbuch   Ammerbach 1571

Obras de Musica   Hernando de Cabezón   1578

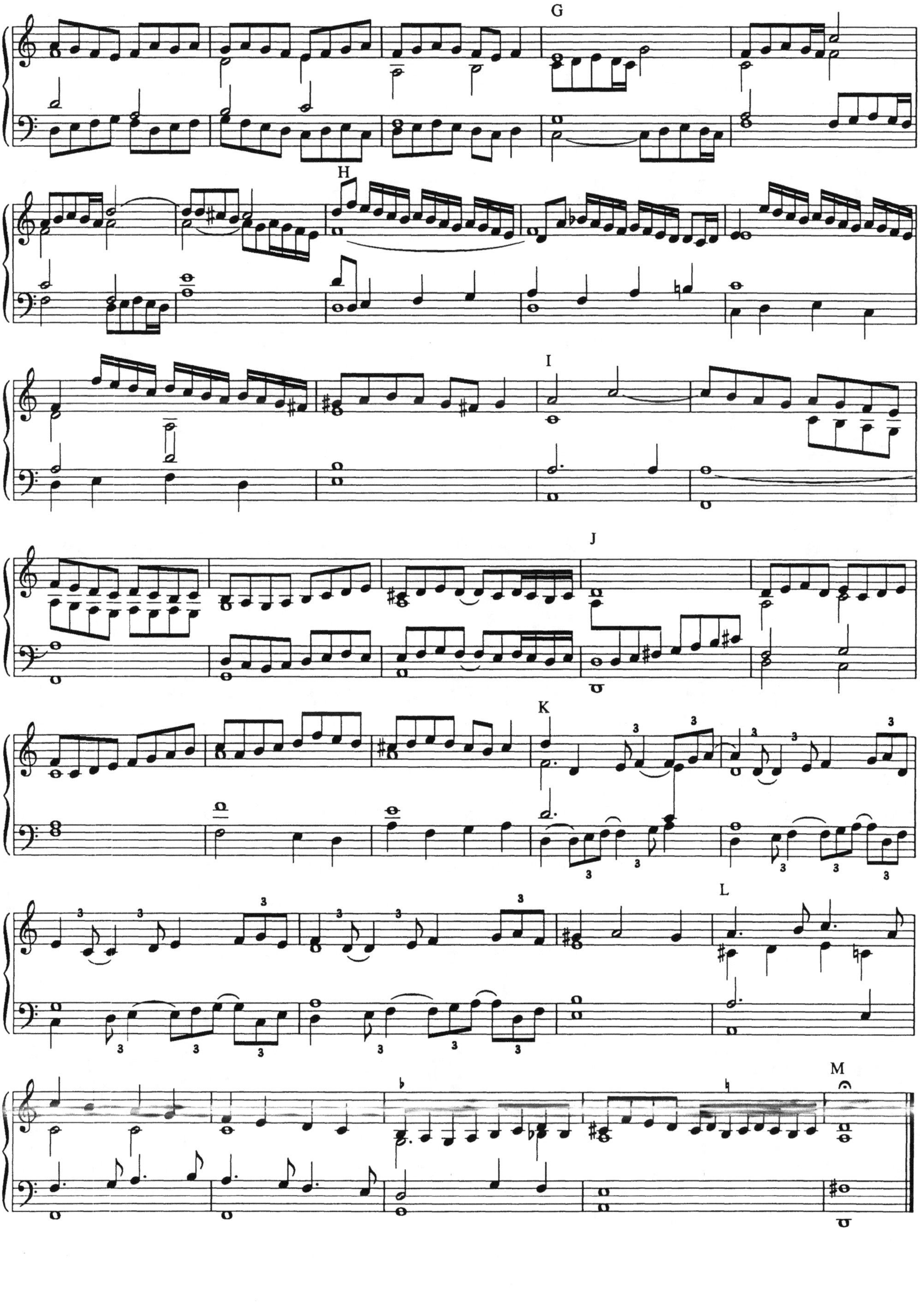
G
H
I
J
K
L
M

Tabulatura   Jan z Lublina 1537-48

50 Trattado de Glosas   Ortiz 1553
Recercada Prima

52

Recercada Segonda

Trattado de Glosas   Ortiz 1553
Recercada Tercera

Trattado de Glosas Ortiz 1553
Recercada Quarta que es una Quinta Boz

64

da sonar con la viola bastarda delle treplicate sola

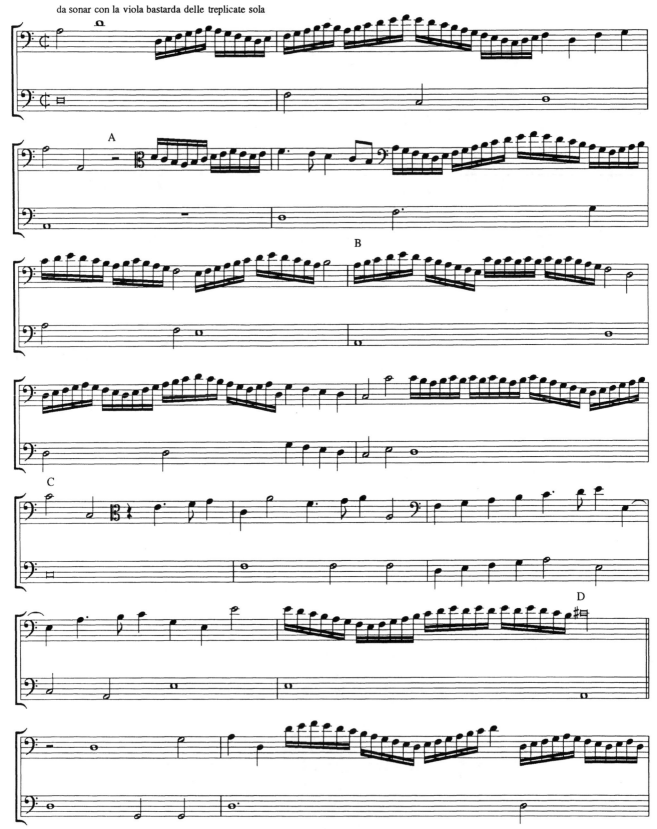

Alcvne Opere di diuersi passagiate da Vicenzo Bonizzi 1626

viola bastarda

70

Georg Rhaw Bicinia II   Pierre de Manchicourt 1545

1er Livre de Chansons à deux parties   Antonio Gardane 1577

Variarum Linguarum Tricinia   Josquin Baston 1560

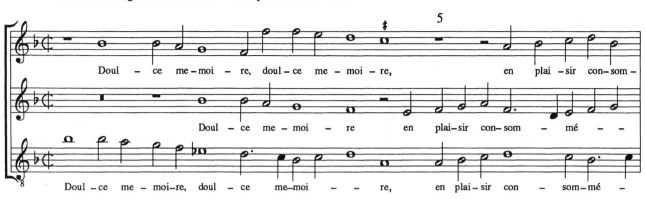

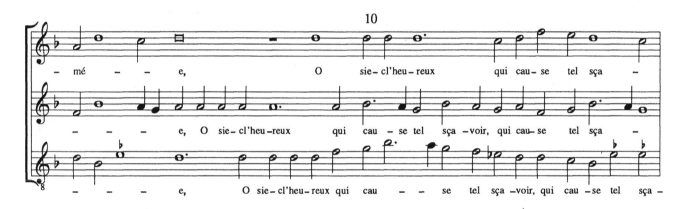

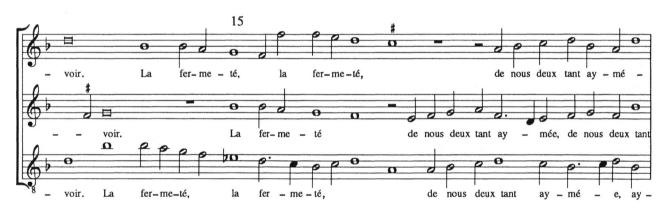

Il Primo Libro de Canzoni Francese a sei voci   Jacques Buus 1543

Magnificat   Clemens non Papa

Performers' Parts

Buus: Il Primo Libro de Canzoni Francese (1)

Soprano I

Doul — ce me-moi — — re

en plai – sir con – som — — — mé — e,

O sie – cl'heu reux   O sie – cl'heu - reux

qui cau-se tel sça — — — — — — voir.

La fer – me - té

de nous deux tant ay – mé – e,

de nous deux tant ay – mé – e,   qui a nos maulx a

sçeu, a sçeu si bien   pour – voir.

98

Buus: Il Primo Libro de Canzoni Francese (2)
Soprano I

Or main-te-nant a per-du son pou-voir, Rom-

-pant le but de ma seul' es-pe-ran-ce,

Ser-vant d'e-xem-ple, ser-vant d'e-xem-ple,

a tous pi-teux a voir.

Fi-ny le bien, le mal sou-dain com-men-ce,

le mal sou-dain com-men-ce,

Fi-ny le bien, le mal sou-dain com-men-

-ce, le mal sou-dain com-men-ce.

Buus: Il Primo Libro de Canzoni Francese (1)

Soprano II

Doul – ce me– moi – – re en plai – sir con– som– mé – –

– – e, en plai – sir con – som – mé – – e,

O sie – cl'heu– reux qui cau– se tel sça – voir, O sie – cl'heu –

– reux qui cau – se tel sça – voir, O sie – cl'heu – reux qui cau – se tel

sça – voir. La fer– me– té de nous deux

tant ay – mé, de nous deux tant ay – mé – –

– e, qui a nos maulx a sçeu si bien pour – voir.

qui a nos maulx, a sçeu si bien pour – voir, qui a nos maulx a sçeu si bien

Bass

Buus: Il Primo Libro de Canzoni Francese (2)

103

Baston: Variarum Linguarum Tricinia

Soprano I

Buus: Il Primo Libro de Canzoni Francese (1)

Baston: Variarum Linguarum Tricinia

Soprano II

Doul - ce me- moi- re en plai - sir con - som - mé -

- - e, O sie- cl'heu- reux qui cau- se tel sça - voir, qui cau- se tel sça -

- - voir. La fer- me- té de nous deux tant ay - mée, de nous deux tant

ay - mée, qui a nos maulx a sçeu si bien pour- voir, a sçeu si bien pour - - voir.

Or main- te - nant a perdu son pouvoir, a perdu son pouvoir, a perdu son pouvoir, a

per- du son pou - voir. Rom- pant le but, rom- pant le but de ma seul' es- pe- ran -

- ce, ser- vant d'ex- em - ple a tous pi- teux a voir, ser - vant d'ex- em - ple, ser -

vant d'ex- em - ple a tous piteux a voir, a tous piteux a voir, a tous piteux a voir, a tous piteux a

voir, a tous pi- teux a voir. Fi - ni le bien, fi - ni le

bien, le mal soudain com- men - - ce, soudain, le mal soudain com - men -

- ce, fi - ni le bien, fi - ni le bien, le mal soudain com- men - -

- ce, soudain, le mal soudain com - men - ce, le mal soudain commen - - ce.

Buus: Il Primo Libro de Canzoni Francese (2)

Alto

Doul - ce me - moi - re, doul - ce me - moi - - re, en plai - sir con - som - mé -

- - e, O sie - cl'heu - reux qui cau - se tel sça - voir, qui cau - se tel sça -

- voir. La fer - me - té, la fer - me - té, de nous deux tant ay - mé - e, ay -

- mé - e, qui a nos maulx a sçeu si bien pour - voir, pour voir, si bien pour voir. Or main - te -

- nant, or main - te - nant, or main - te - nant, or main - - - te - nant, a perdu son pouvoir, a perdu son pouvoir, a

- per - du son pou - voir, Rom - pant le but de ma seul' es - - pe - ran - ce,

rom - pant le but de ma seul' es - pe - ran - ce, ser - vant d'ex - em - ple,

ser - vant d'ex - em - ple a tous piteux a voir, ser - vant d'ex - em - ple, ser - vant d'ex - em - ple a

tous pi - teux a voir. Fi - ni le bien, fi - ni le bien, fi - ni le bien le, mal sou -

- dain, mal sou - dain, le mal soudain, le mal soudain, le mal soudain commen - ce,

fi - ni le bien, fi - ni le bien, le mal soudain, mal sou - dain, le mal soudain, le

mal soudain, le mal soudain com - men - ce, com - men - ce.

Buus: Il Primo Libro de Canzoni Francese (1)

Doul — ce me – moi — re   en plai – sir con – som –

– – – mé — — e,   en plai – sir con – som-

– mé — e,   O sie – cl'heu – reux qui cau – se tel sça – –

– – – – – – voir.

La fer – me – té   de

deux tant   ay – mé – e,   de

nous deux tant ay – mé – e,   qui a nos maulx a sçeu, a sçeu,

si bien   pour – voir.

Clemens non Papa: Magnificat

Soprano

Si – cut e – rat si – cut e – – rat si –

– cut e – – – rat in prin – ci – pi – o et nunc et

sem – – per et in sae – cu – la sae – cu – lo – rum a – men

et in sae – cu – la sae – cu – lo – rum a – – – –

– – men et in sae – cu – la sae – cu – – lo

– – rum a – – – – – – – men.

Buus: Il Primo Libro de Canzoni Francese (2)

Or main – te – nant a per – du son pou – voir, Rom –

– pant le but de ma seul' es – pe – ran – ce,

Ser – vant d'e – xem – ple, ser – vant d'e – xem – ple

a tous pi – teux a voir Fi –

– ny le bien, le mal sou – dain com – men – ce,

le mal sou – dain com – men – ce. Fi –

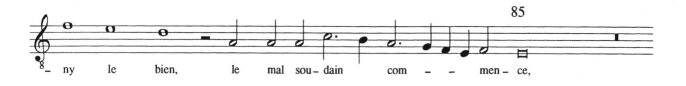

– ny le bien, le mal sou – dain com – men – ce,

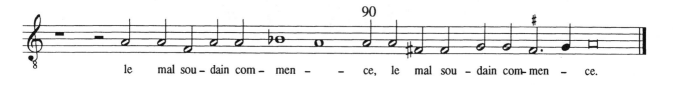

le mal sou – dain com – men – ce, le mal sou – dain com – men – ce.

Alto

Si – cut e – rat (si – cut e – – – rat) in

prin – ci – pi – o et nunc et sem –per (et nunc et sem – per) et nunc et

sem – per et in sae – cu – la sae – cu – lo – rum a – –

– – men sae – cu – lo – rum a – men (sae – cu – lo – rum a – – men) et in sae – cu –

–la sae – cu – lo – rum a – men sae – cu – lo – rum a – men et in

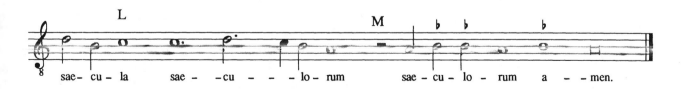

sae – cu – la sae – cu – – lo – rum sae – cu – lo – rum a – – men.

Buus: Il Primo Libro de Canzoni Francese (1)

Bass I

Doul _ _ _ ce, doul _ce, me _ moi _ _ re en plai _ sir

con _ som _ mé _ _ e, en plai _ sir con _ som _ mé _ e, en plai _ sir con _ som _

mé _ _ _ _ e. O sie _ cl'heu _ reux

qui cau _ se tel sça _ voir, qui cau _ _ se tel sça _

_ voir. La fer _ me _ té, La fer _ me _ té de

nous deux tant ay _ mé _ _ e, de nous deux tant ay _ mé _ e, de nous deux tant ay _

_ mé _ _ _ _ e, qui a nos maulx

a sçeu si bien pour _ voir, a sçeu si bien pour _ voir. Or main te _

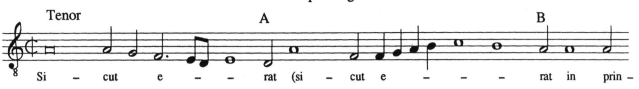

Tenor

Si — cut e — rat (si — cut e — rat in prin —

— ci — pi — o et nunc et sem — per et nunc et sem — per et

nunc et sem — per) et in sae — cu — la sae — cu — lo — rum a — — — men

et in sae — cu — la sae — cu — lo — rum a — — — — —

— men et in sae — cu — la sae — cu — lo — rum a — —

— — men a — — — — — men.

Buus: Il Primo Libro de Canzoni Francese (2)

Bass I

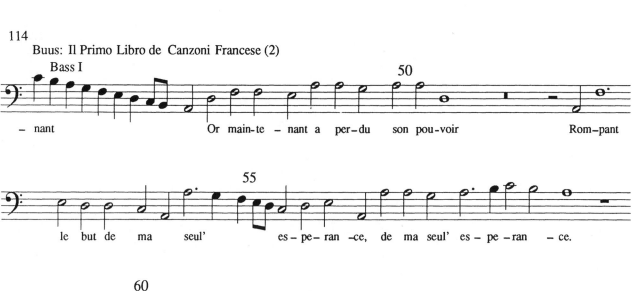

— nant   Or main-te — nant a per-du   son pou-voir   Rom—pant

le   but de   ma   seul'   es—pe — ran —ce,   de ma seul' es — pe —ran   —   ce.

Ser — vant d'e — xem   —   ple, ser—vant d'e   —   xem—ple a   tous pi —teux a   voir,   a

tous   pi—teux a   voir. Fi — ny   le   bien,   fi — ny   le   bien,

fi — ny   le   bien, le   mal sou — dain,   le   mal sou —

— dain com — men   —   ce,   le   mal   sou — dain com — men   —   ce,

fi — ny   le   bien, le   mal sou — dain,

le   mal sou — dain, le   mal sou — dain, sou—dain, com— men   —   —   ce.

Bass I

Si — — cut e — — rat in

prin – ci — — — pi – o et nunc et sem – per (et nunc et sem –

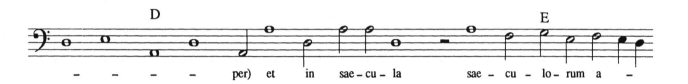

– — — — — per) et in sae – cu – la sae – cu – lo – rum a –

– — men sae – cu – lo – rum a – men (sae – cu – lo – rum

a – men) sae – cu – lo – rum a – men et in

sae – cu – la sae – cu – lo – rum a – men sae – cu – lo – — rum a – men.

Buus: Il Primo Libro de Canzoni Francese (1)

Bass II

Doul — — ce, doul — ce, me-moi — re en plai-sir con-som-mé-

— — — — e, en plai — sir con -som-mé —

— — — e, O sie – cl'heu – reux, O sie– cl'heu -reux, O

sie – cl'heu – reux, qui cau — se, qui

cau-se tel sça-voir. La fer — — me — té, la fer-me-

– té de nous deux tant ay – mé — e, la fer – me –

– té de nous deux tant ay – mé — e, qui a nos maulx,

qui a nos maulx, a sçeu si bien, a

Bass II

Si — cut e — rat in prin — — ci — pi — o si — cut

e — rat in prin — ci — pi — o et nunc et sem — — —

— — per et in sae — cu — la sae — cu — lo — rum a — — men

sae — cu — lo — rem a — men et in sae — cu — la sae — cu — lo — rum a — men

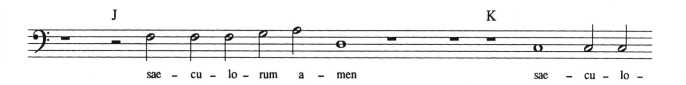

sae — cu — lo — rum a — men sae — cu — lo —

— rum a — men (et in sae — cu — la sae — cu — lo — rum a — — men.)

Buus: Il Primo Libro de Canzoni Francese (2)

Bass II

sçeu si bien pour – voir, or main–te – nant a per–du son pou–voir. Rom–pant le

but, rom–pant le but, rom – pant le but, de ma seul' es –pe –

– ran–ce, Ser – vant d'e– xem – ple a tous pi –teux a

voir, a tous pi – teux a voir. Fi – ny

le bien, le mal sou – dain com – men – ce,

le mal sou – dain com – men – – – ce, Fi – ny

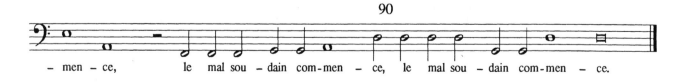

le bien, le mal sou – dain com –

– men – ce, le mal sou – dain com–men – ce, le mal sou – dain com–men – ce.

Trattado de Glosas   Ortiz 1553
Recercada Prima

Trattado de Glosas   Ortiz 1553
          Recercada Segonda

Trattado de Glosas   Ortiz 1553
Recercada Tercera

Trattado de Glosas   Ortiz 1553

Recercada Quarta que es una Quinta Boz

Dalla Casa: Il vero modo di diminuir (1)

da sonar con la viola bastarda delle treplicate sola

Bonizzi: Alcvne Opere di diuersi passagiate (1)

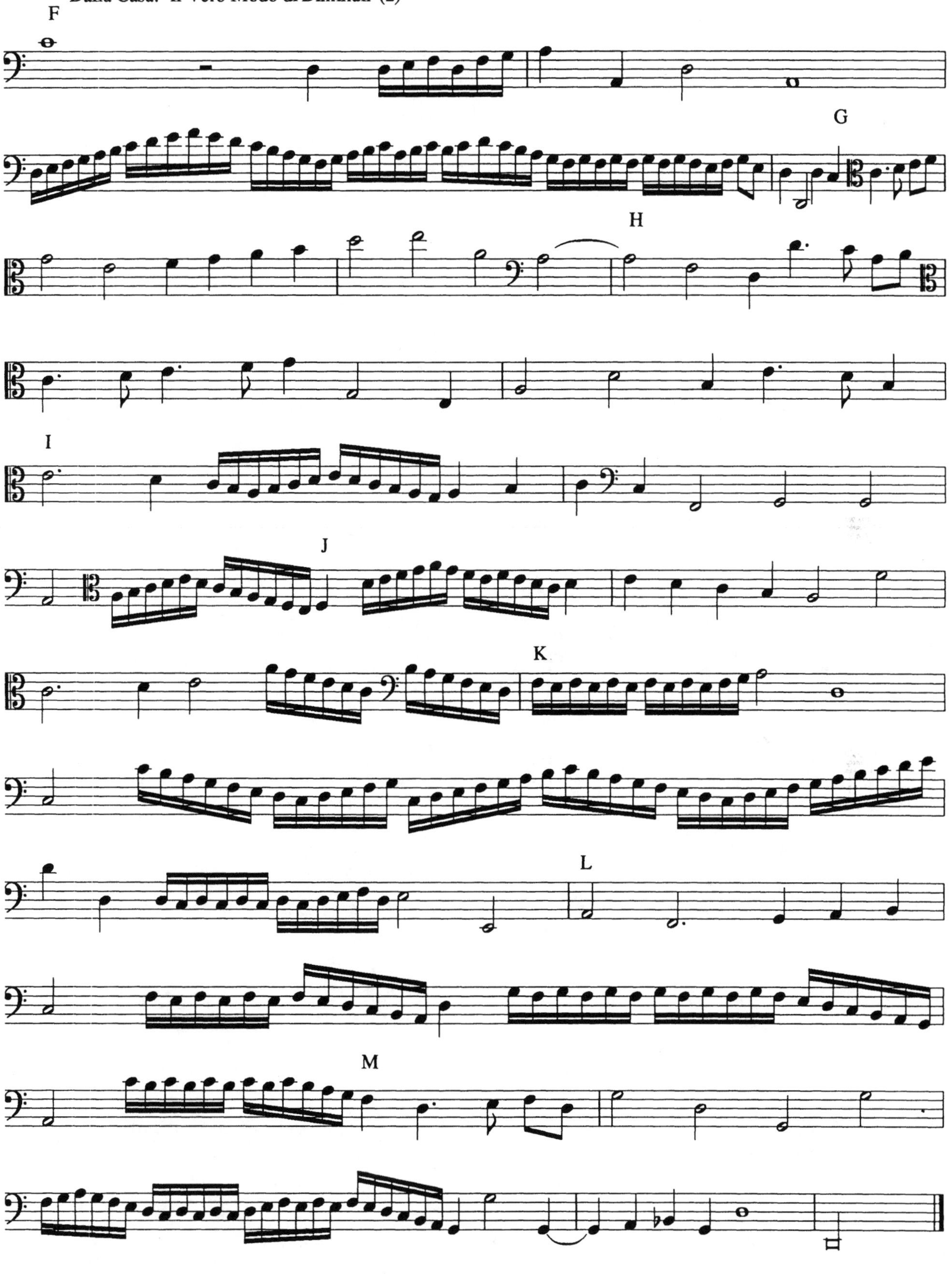
F
G
H
I
J
K
L
M

Bonizzi: Alcvne opere di diversi passegiate (3)

Bibliography of *Doulce memoire*

Settings à 4

Le Parangon des chansons contenant plusieurs nouvelles et delectables chansons que oncques ne furent imprimees. . . . Lyon: Jacques Moderne, 1537 or 1538. \1 vol. in 8vo obl.

Sixiesme livre contenant XXVII chansons nouvelles a quatre parties en deux volumes. Paris: Attaingnant, 1539. \2 vols. in 8vo obl.

Second livre contenant XXVII chansons nouvelles. . . . Paris: Attaingnant et H. Jullet, 1540. \2 vols. in 8vo obl.

Le second livre des chansons a quatre parties auquel sont contenues trente et une chansons convenables tant a la voix comme aux instruments. . . . Antwerp: T. Susato, 1544. \4 vols. in 8vo obl.

Premier livre des chansons esleues en nombre XXX, pour les meilleures et plus frequentes, es cours des princes, convenables a tous instrumentz musicaulz. Paris: Attaingnant, 1549. \2 vols. in 8vo obl.

Premier livre du recueil contenant XXX chansons anciennes, a quatre parties en un volume, les meilleures et plus excellentes (et les plus convenables aux instrumens). . . . Paris: N. du Chemin, 1551. \1 vol. in 4to obl.

Trattado de glosas sobre clausulas y otros generos de puntos en la musica de violones nuevamente puestos en luz, de Diego Ortiz tolledano. Rome: 1553. Modern edition, edited by Max Schneider, Kassel: Bärenreiter-Verlag, 1936.

Jardin musical, contenant plusieurs belles fleures de chansons . . .le tiers livre. Antwerp: H. Waelrant & J. Laet, 1556. \4 vols. in 4to obl.

Septiesme livre des chansons a quatre parties, de nouveau reveu corrige et de plusieurs autres nouvelles chansons. . . . Louvain: P. Phalese, 1570. \4 vols. in 4to obl.

Musica di diversi autori. . . . Venice: Angelo Gardano, 1577. In score.

Livre septieme des chansons a quatre parties nouvellement recorrige, et augmente de plusieurs chansons, non imprimes auparavant, accomodees tant aux instruments, comme a la voix. . . . Antwerp: veuve J. Bellere, 1597. \4 vol in 8vo obl.

Livre septieme des chansons vulgaires de diverses auteurs a quatre parties. . . . Antwerp: P. Phalese, 1609. \4 vols. in 4to obl.

Basel, Universitätsbibliothek, Mss. F.X. 17-20.

Basel, Universitätsbibliothek, Mss. F.X. 22-24.

Basel, Universitätsbibliothek, Mss. F.IX 59-62.

Regensburg, Proske-Bibliothek, Cod. C.120; Ms. A.R.940/41.

Intabulations for Lute

Pierre de Teghi, *Des chansons et motetz reduitz en tablature de luc, a quatre, cincque et six parties, livre troisieme. Composees par l'excellent maistre Pierre de Teghi padouan.* Louvain: P. Phalese, 1547. 1 vol. in 8vo obl. Same as *Carminum ad testudinis usum compositorum, liber tertius,* 1547.

Hans Newsidler, *Das Ander Buch / Ein new kuenstlich Lauten Buch.* . . . Nürnberg, 1549.

Carminum quae chely vel testudine canuntur, liber primus. Cum brevi introductione in usum testudinis. Louvain: P. Phalese, 1549.

Hortus musarum in quo tanquam flosculi quidam selectissimorum carminum collecti sunt ex optimis quibusque autoribus. . . . Louvain: P. Phalese, 1552. Same as Teghi, *Des Chansons* (above), except that the lowest string is not tuned down a step in this version. Also same as *Thesaurus Musicus.* . . . Louvain: P. Phalese, 1552.

Benedict de Drusina, *Tabulatura continens insignes et selectissimas quasdam fantasias: cantiones germanicas, italicas, ac gallicas: passamezo: choreas & mutetas*. . . . per Benedictum de Drusina elbigensem. Frankfurt: J. Eichorn, 1556.

Wolff Heckel, *Discant Lautten Buch, von mancherley schoenen und lieblichen stucken*. Strassburg: Wyss, 1556.

Albert de Rippe, *Tiers livre de tabelature de luth contenant plusieurs chansons*. Paris: A. le Roy et R. Ballard, 1562. Same as *Thesaurus musicus*. Louvain: P. Phalese, 1573.

Luculentum Theatrum Musicum. . . . Louvain: P. Phalese, 1568. Same as *Theatrum Musicum*. Louvain: Phalese & Bellere, 1571.

Mathaeum Waisselium, *Tabulatura continens insignes et selectissimas quasque Cantiones*. . . . in luceam aedita. Frankfurt a.d. Oder: J. Eichorn, 1573.

Munich, Bayerische Staatsbibliothek, Mus. Ms. 266, nos. 59 and 92.

Munich, Bayerische Staatsbibliothek, Mus. Ms. 2987, no.36.

Intabulations for Cittern

Sebastian Vreedman, *Nova longeque elegantissima cithara ludenda carmina*. . . . Louvain: P. Phalese, 1568. Same as *Hortulus cytharae, in duos distinctus libros*. . . . Louvain: P. Phalese; Antwerp: J. Bellere, 1570.

Sixt Kargel, *Renovata cythera*. . . . Strassburg: bei Bernhard Jobin, 1578.

Intabulations for Keyboard

Hernando de Cabezón, *Obras de Musica*, 1578, in *Hispaniae schola musica sacra*, vol. VII, edited by Felipe Pedrell. Barcelona, 1897; New York: Johnson Reprint, 1971. Pp. 17-19.

Cracow, Biblioteka Jagiellonska, Ms. 1716 ("Jan of Lublin Tablature") 1537-48, fol. 197v.

Elias Nicolaus Ammerbach, *Orgel oder Instrument Tabulaturbuch*. . . . Nürnberg, 1583.

Arrangements for Viola da Gamba

Diego Ortiz, *Trattado de glosas* 1553 (See above, under Settings à 4.)

Girolamo Dalla Casa, *Il vero modo di diminuir*. . . . Venice, 1584.

Vicenzo Bonizzi, *Alcvne opere di diversi avtori a diversi voci passaggiate principalmente per la viola bastarda*. . . . Venice: Vincente, 1626.

Other Arrangements Based on Sandrin's Chanson

François de Layolle, *Le Parangon des chansons quart livre contenant XXII chansons a deux et a troys parties*. . . . Lyon: J. Moderne, 1539.

Pierre de Manchicourt, *Secundus tomus bicinorum, quae et ipsa sunt gallica, latina, germanica ex praestantissimus sympohonistis collecta*. . . . Wittenberg: G. Rhaw, 1545.

Antonio Gardane, *Premier livre de chansons a deux parties composees par plusieurs autheurs*. Paris: le Roy et R. Ballard, 1578.

Josquin Baston, *Vararium linguarum tricinis a praestantissimus musicis. . . tomi secundi*. Nürnberg: J. von Berg & U. Neuber, 1560.

Munich, Bayerische Staatsbibliothek, Mus. Ms 1502.

Jacques Buus, *Il primo libro di canzoni francese a 6 voci*. . . . Venice: Gardano, 1543.

Contrafactum and Parody Masses

Jacobus Clemens non papa, *Magnificat primi toni* (sicut erat à 5). Reprinted in Clemens Opera, vol. IV.

Cipriano de Rore, *Missa super dulcis memoria* (1566), in *Collected Works*, edited by Bernhard Meier, vol. VII, pp. 122-48.

Orlando di Lasso, *Missa ad imitationem moduli Doulce memoire*, (1577), in *Sämtliche Werke*, edited by Siegfried Hermelink, Neue Reihe, Band 4: Messen 10-17.